All can be viewed from the splendid elevated promenade provided by the most complete circuit of city walls in England, as well as explored more closely.

Attractively set on the River Dee, Chester has an ancient history dating back to its days as a Roman port and fortress. Its once strategic importance as a seaport is reflected in its Lord Mayor's cou... of the Dee', and t... son still holds the ... reflecting the city'... defending the onc... with Wales.

Chester is the m... in north-west England, as rich in architectural heritage as it is unique in character.

and seventeenth centuries or more modern interpretations such as St Michael's Buildings pictured here, built early this century.

HISTORY

History

The ancient city of Chester, its name derived from the Latin castra, or camp, was established on the River Dee as a Roman fortress in about AD 79. Its site, on a low sandstone plateau within a bend in the river, was chosen as the point where the river could most easily be bridged and as a protected harbour for sea-going ships.

Deva Castra, or Deva – its Roman name was taken from the river – proved to be of strategic importance against attacks from marauding Welsh tribes from the west and the Celtic Brigantes from the north, and also against later Irish attack. The fortress, headquarters of one of three Roman legions in Britain, is believed to have contained up to 6,000 soldiers. There is still evidence of the Roman occupation in the city, which retains its grid-like street pattern and has remains of an amphitheatre, the harbour wall and the defensive wall of the fortress.

The harbour was where the racecourse known as the Roodee is now, and Chester was a major trading centre and port, importing wines and exporting salt from Cheshire and minerals from North Wales and Anglesey. But by 383 the Roman legions had withdrawn and Chester seems to have been virtually deserted for a considerable period.

ABOVE **In the Roman Garden just outside Newgate, Roman remains include the columns of a legionary bathhouse. There is also a reconstruction of a Roman hypocaust heating system.**

BELOW **This model shows how the Roman fortress of Deva might have looked, viewed looking west with the Welsh hills in the background. The line of the main streets, from north to south and east to west, is evident today.**

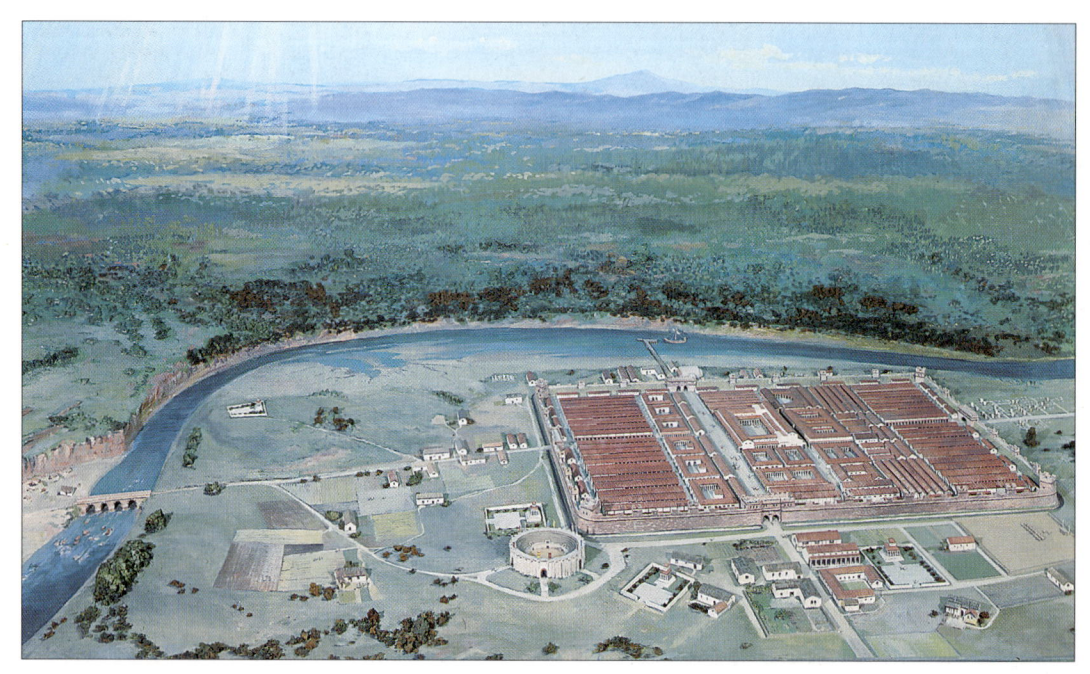

HISTORY

It eventually flourished again under Aethelflaeda, daughter of Alfred the Great and 'Lady of the Mercians', who re-established it as a fortress against the Danes and against further raids from the Welsh and more Vikings from across the Irish Sea. By 937 Chester had become politically important enough for King Edgar, the first king of all England, to have himself rowed on the River Dee to the town by eight Celtic kings as a sign of their subservience to him.

Frequent Viking raids during the next century resulted in economic decline which was reversed only after the Norman Conquest when William the Conqueror built a powerful castle so he could subdue local Saxons and defend against the troublesome Welsh. William's nephew, known as 'Hugh the Wolf', became Earl of Chester, a feared leader who further developed the fortifications and pacified an extensive area around the city to such good effect that it prospered as trade expanded. In 1092 he turned his attention to more spiritual matters and founded a great Benedictine abbey, whose church later became Chester's cathedral.

As the medieval period progressed the old Roman walls were extended to protect the town. Chester was now the principal port for north-west England, and its wine trade with the south of France was especially important. It became a city in 1300

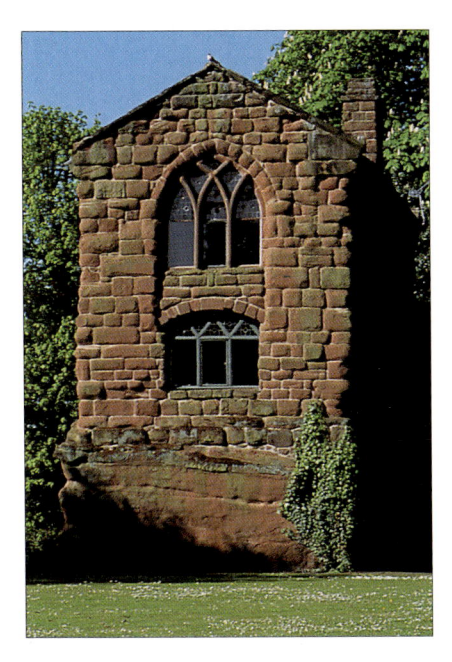

LEFT According to local legend, the Anchorite's Cell, a sandstone building to the north of the Groves, was the last home of the Saxon King Harold, who – so the story goes – survived the battle of Hastings in 1066 to live as a holy hermit or anchorite in Chester.

LEFT Medieval Chester Castle, whose gatehouse is shown in this eighteenth-century painting, was almost entirely demolished in the late eighteenth century to make way for a new complex of buildings. The original Norman castle was probably of timber construction and it was rebuilt in stone with outer defensive walls in the thirteenth century.

HISTORY

ABOVE **This impressive medieval crypt, with vaulted arches supported on substantial columns, survives in the lower level of one of Chester's medieval Rows. Now a wine bar in Watergate Street, it is one of a number of such crypts in the city.**

when Edward I granted a charter giving rights of self-government, and its markets and fairs became increasingly famous. It was from this period that Chester's famous Rows, streets of galleried shops, originate, as well as the mystery plays, biblical stories which were staged in the streets by the increasingly powerful and wealthy guilds who regulated trade.

By 1550, despite the silting up of the river and the damage caused by several serious fires and outbreaks of plague, Chester was still a reasonably prosperous port. But in the Civil War as a royalist city it was heavily bombarded and damaged by the parliamentarians. Its citizens were under siege for about a year and four months, reduced to eating dogs, cats and rats before being starved into surrender.

In the late seventeenth century they began to rebuild their shattered city. The growth of turnpikes and stage coaching, together with new industries, all helped the city to flourish. Communications were further improved by the opening of the canal to Nantwich in 1779 and by rail links to Shrewsbury, Crewe, Birkenhead and North Wales in the 1840s. Chester became a fashionable area, and in Victorian times much of

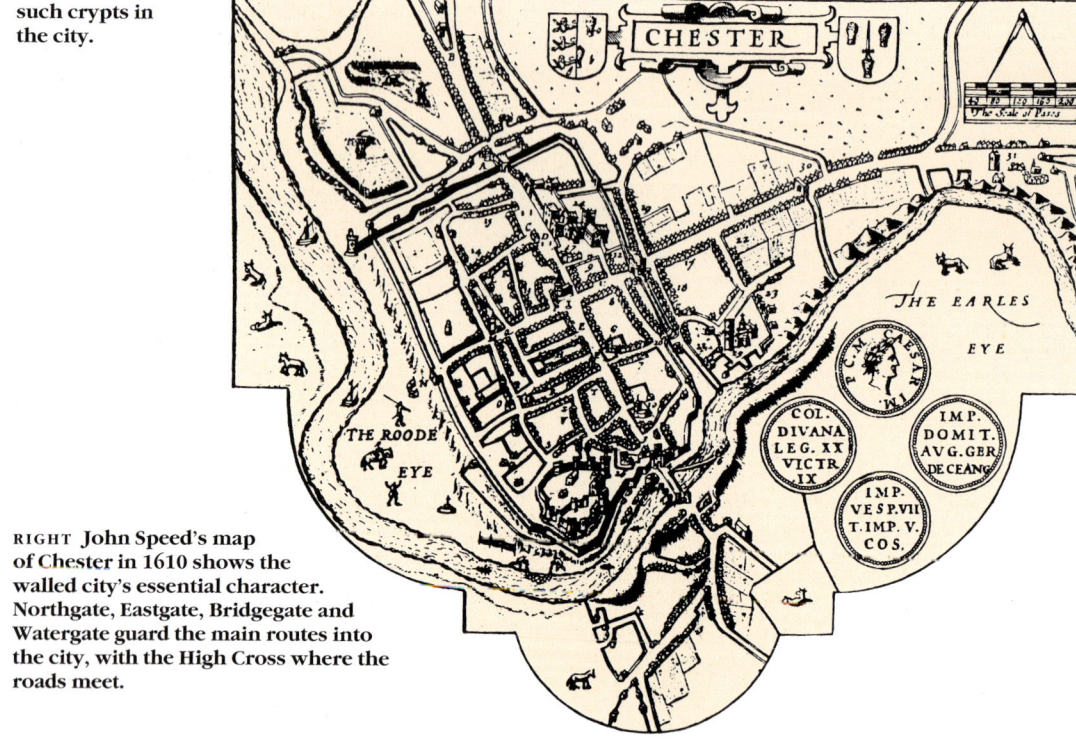

RIGHT **John Speed's map of Chester in 1610 shows the walled city's essential character. Northgate, Eastgate, Bridgegate and Watergate guard the main routes into the city, with the High Cross where the roads meet.**

HISTORY

ABOVE **This modern painting of the Civil War siege of Chester shows the ramparts behind the city walls at Abbey Green being reinforced. The citizens held out for well over a year until starvation forced them to surrender.**

the city was rebuilt, restored or remodelled in half-timbered style, creating its distinctive 'black and white' appearance. The ancient Rows were preserved as medieval architecture became appreciated. Today Chester is a thriving commercial, administrative, cultural and tourist centre, attracting visitors from all over the world.

BELOW **Chester's railway station, opened in 1848, was built by the four railway companies that then served the city. Designed in Italianate style, it was one of the largest stations in the country at that time.**

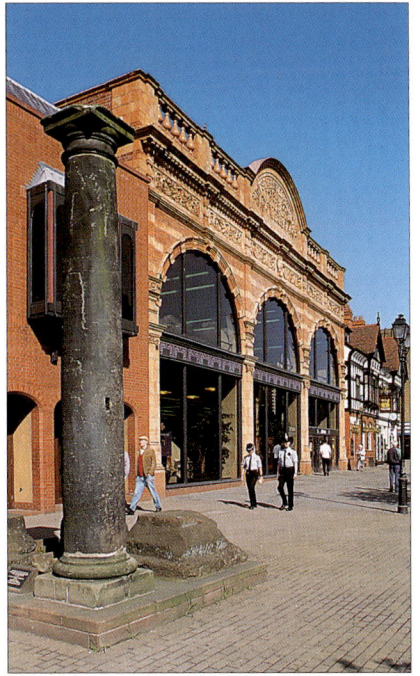

ABOVE **Chester's architecture reflects the city's rich history. Here an elegant Edwardian façade is incorporated into the modern library, while the eighteenth-century pillar outside, from the neo-classical period, is flanked by the bases of three Roman columns.**

WALLS AND GATES

Walls and gates

Chester's walls and gates form a virtually unbroken two-mile (3 km) circuit of the city. The walls are up to six feet (1.8 m) wide and at times rise to forty feet (12 m) above street level, with superb views from them of bustling streets, the river and the canal, and panoramas of the Welsh hills. The gates, formerly entrances to the city, are now splendid archways over busy roads.

The walls were developed into an attractive city promenade in the eighteenth century. Daniel Defoe wrote in 1724 of 'a very pleasant walk round the city, upon the walls, and within the battlements, from whence you may see the country round'.

LEFT A superb traffic-free zone is formed by the walkway along the walls. From it many of the more spectacular buildings can be seen from a different angle.

BELOW The Eastgate was built as a bridge in 1769 to replace the original medieval entrance which dated back to at least the twelfth century. The splendid clock was added to commemorate Queen Victoria's diamond jubilee in 1897.

WALLS AND GATES

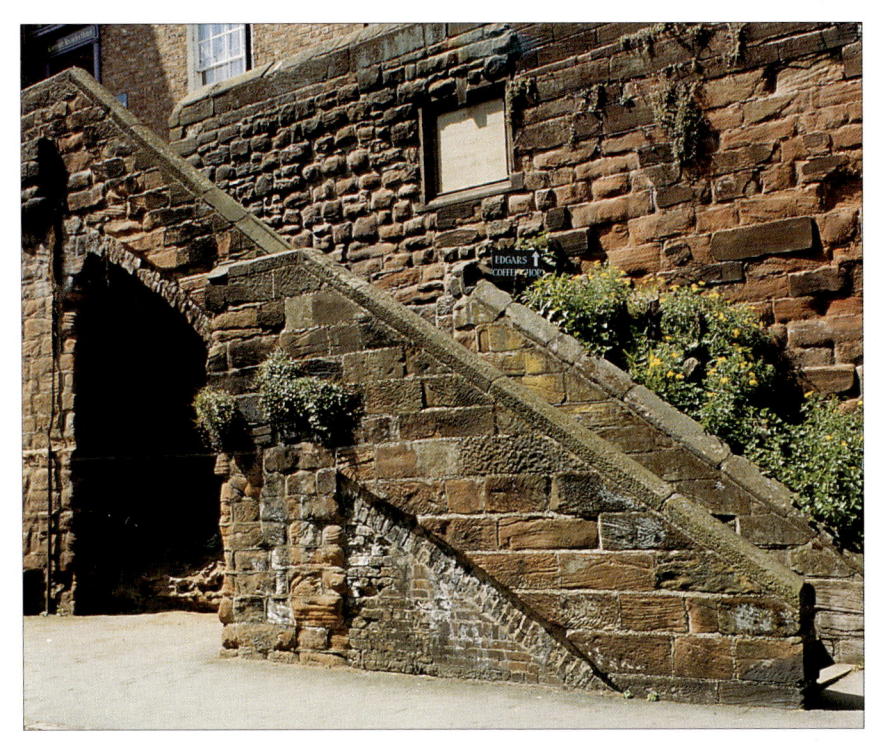

LEFT The Recorder's Steps were built against the walls by an eighteenth-century Chester judge to give him easy access to the river from his house above. Built into the walls nearby are the Wishing Steps which are supposed to grant the wish of anyone able to run up and down them without pausing for breath – though older sources claim that it is necessary to run up, down and up again for the desired result!

Turf and timber ramparts had encircled the original Roman fortress but these were twice rebuilt in stone by the Romans. The Anglo-Saxon kings of Mercia extended them to their present shape and a number of defensive towers and gateways were added later. Today's walls date mainly from the thirteenth century, but they were rebuilt and repaired many times for defensive purposes before being made into a promenade. They can be joined by steps at several points, including all the main city gates.

For centuries Old Dee Bridge was the only direct route from Wales into Chester. Bridgegate, or the Welsh Gate as it was sometimes called, was massively fortified in medieval times to protect the citizens from possible Welsh attack. The present Bridgegate with its stone balustrades dates from 1782.

Although all the medieval gates were pulled down in the late eighteenth and early nineteenth centuries to allow traffic to flow more

LEFT The elaborate, colourful Eastgate Clock is one of Chester's famous landmarks. From where it stands on the Eastgate, on the walls walkway, there is a splendid view of the busy shopping streets. The clock's supporting ironwork was designed by the architect John Douglas, who designed many of Chester's black-and-white buildings.

WALLS AND GATES

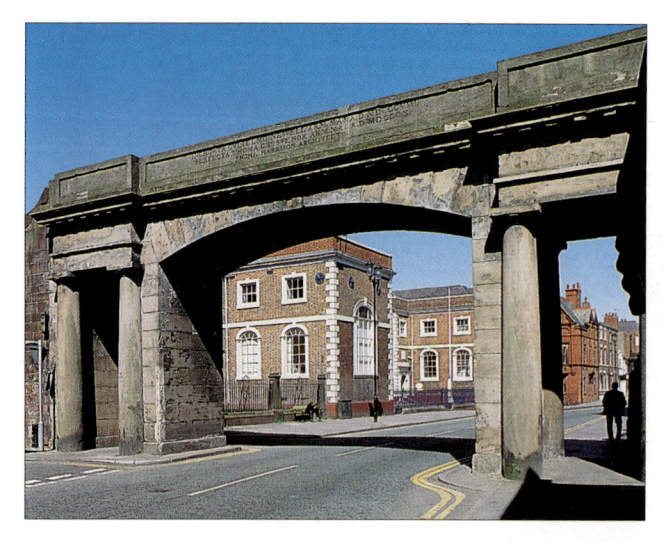

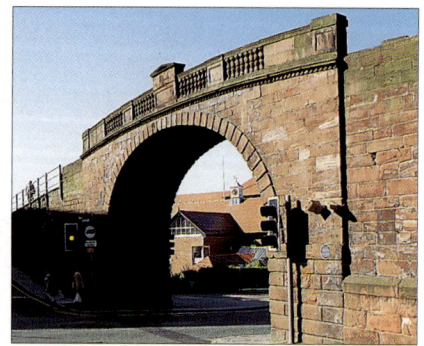

ABOVE The Watergate was built in 1788, but an earlier gate on the site was in medieval times close to the River Dee and cargoes unloaded from ships were brought through it into the city.

ABOVE The Northgate, built by Thomas Harrison in the early nineteenth century in neoclassical style, replaced a medieval gate defended by towers, portcullis and drawbridge.

RIGHT King Charles' Tower contains a small display on the Civil War in Chester. It is from here that Charles I is said to have watched the retreat of his defeated army after the battle of Rowton Moor.

easily, replacement gates in the form of bridges were provided so that the walk round the walls would not be interrupted. Newgate, one of the two modern gates in Chester, was built in 1938 as a stone archway flanked by a tower on either side. Next to it is the Wolf Gate, the oldest of the surviving gates, which was rebuilt in the 1760s. The most recent gate is St Martin's Gate, built across the city's inner ring road in 1966. Sadly no bridge was built where the Grosvenor Road breaches the walls, by the castle.

The Kaleyards Gate enshrines an ancient right dating from 1275 granted by Edward I. The monks of the Benedictine abbey of St Werburgh had the right to breach the walls in order to reach their 'kale', or vegetable garden. The gate is still controlled by the cathedral authorities and must be closed at 9 pm.

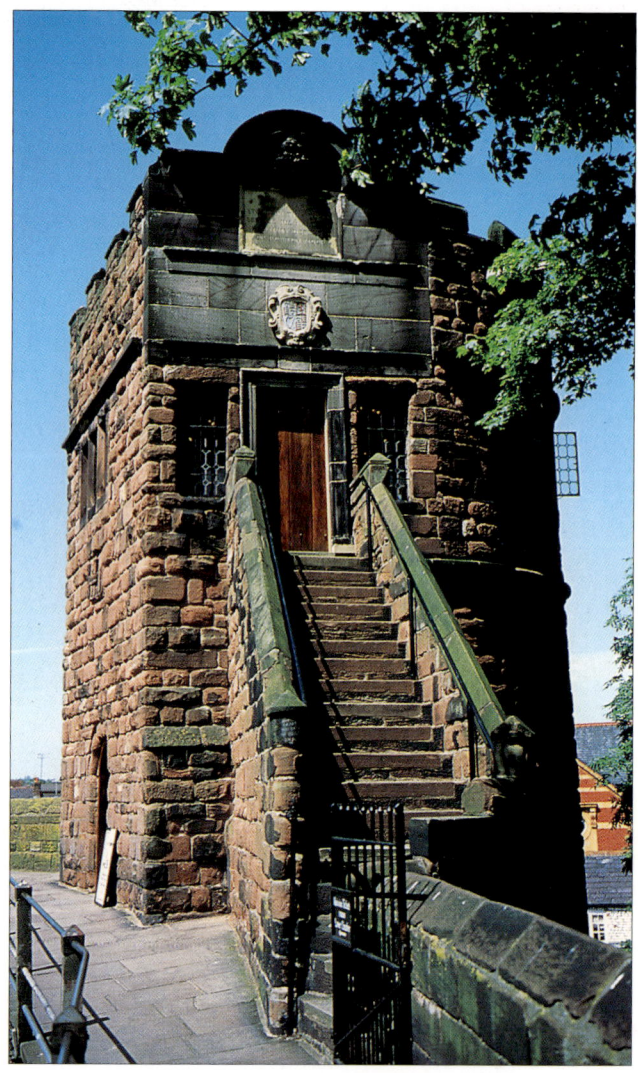

WALLS AND GATES

The towers on the walls have fascinating stories. Standing high above the Chester Canal, King Charles' Tower is built on the foundations of one of Chester's original Roman towers and used to be known as the Phoenix Tower, the phoenix being the emblem of the Guild of Painters, Glaziers, Embroiderers and Stationers who used it as their headquarters. From this vantage point Charles I is said to have watched his defeated royalist army retreating from the battle of Rowton Moor.

At the north-west corner of the defences is Bonewaldesthorne's Tower – a name which it has had since the thirteenth century. It used to stand in the river guarding the harbour, but as the Dee silted up and the harbour moved further away from the walls, a new tower known as the Water Tower, with water on three sides, became part of the defences.

RIGHT **Bonewaldesthorne's Tower originally stood in the river as part of Chester's fortifications on the west, until the River Dee began to silt up.**

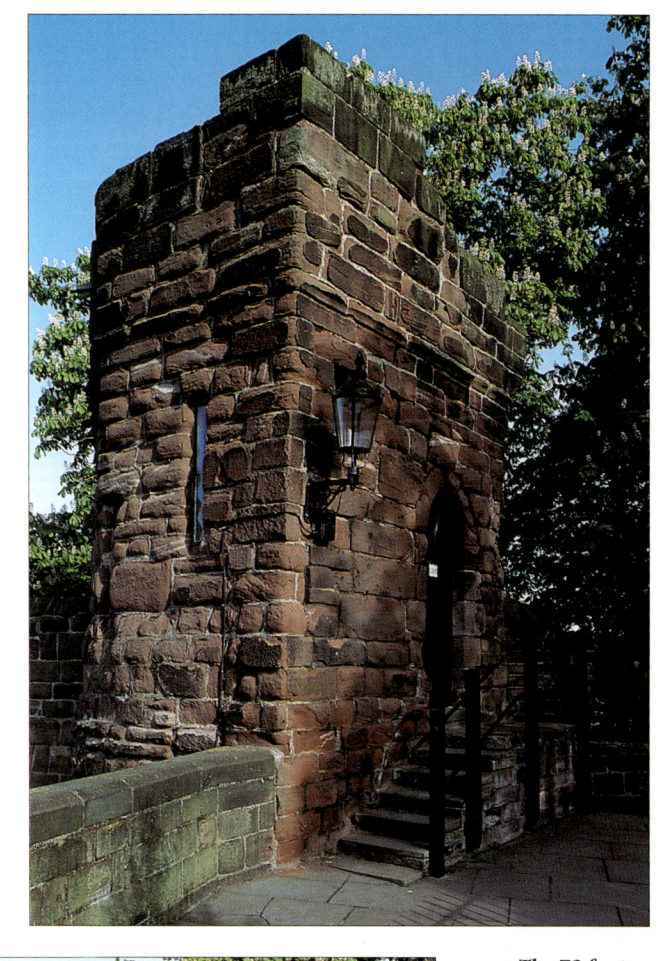

LEFT **The 72-foot-high Water Tower, built for £100 in 1322 when it was almost surrounded by the River Dee, provided an effective defence until the fifteenth century, when the gradual silting up of the river left the tower land-locked. It is now several hundred yards from the river and contains a small museum.**

Black-and-white buildings

Numerous black-and-white buildings provide a visual feast in the centre of Chester. Their gables, oversailing storeys, intricate carvings and small leaded window panes offer fine detail to admire near at hand, while their striking two-tone contrast brings whole streets dramatically to life.

Most of them date from the second half of the nineteenth and early part

RIGHT Eastgate Street has some fine black-and-white buildings. This section has large-scale Victorian buildings juxtaposed with a compact seventeenth-century inn.

BELOW Dating from 1664, the Bear and Billet is a splendid example of a timber-framed town house. It was owned by the earls of Shrewsbury until the nineteenth century. At one time goods would have been hoisted through the door in the gable for storage.

ABOVE Ye Olde King's Head in Lower Bridge Street is an impressive seventeenth-century building with an overhanging upper storey. A sword found under the floorboards in the 1930s when the pub was being renovated is now displayed inside.

BLACK-AND-WHITE BUILDINGS

of the twentieth centuries but many are from the sixteenth and seventeenth centuries. The original buildings were timber framed, with the timberwork arranged in a variety of ways and additional timber often added to form decorative patterns. They had thatched roofs but by 1671 the thatch proved to be such a fire risk that it caused the city authorities to decree that all houses must have tile or slate roofs.

By the beginning of the eighteenth century the town's 'mostly timber buildings' observed by the seventeenth-century traveller Celia Fiennes were increasingly rebuilt or replaced by red brick and stone houses typical of Georgian times. Timber, particularly oak from the Cheshire plain, had become increasingly scarce and expensive.

But black-and-white buildings returned again in Victorian times when it became fashionable to rebuild in half-timbered Tudor style. The Victorian version, though, was often on a much larger scale, and it was usually built of brick, with timber applied only to the façade. It was fashionable then to paint

ABOVE LEFT
Stanley Palace in Watergate Street, built in the late sixteenth century, was once the town house of the Stanley family, of Alderley. It was restored this century. The carving (ABOVE) is on one of the timbers.

ABOVE **The ornate carvings on Bishop Lloyd's House in Watergate Street, the home of the seventeenth-century Bishop of Chester, display fine workmanship. The top picture shows Adam and Eve, and the bottom picture has grotesque figures.**

BLACK-AND-WHITE BUILDINGS

the timber both as a preservative and to make façades look even more attractive.

Although the nineteenth-century Tudor-style buildings make a dramatic impact, it is the carefully restored houses of the fifteenth, sixteenth and seventeenth centuries that are the most celebrated. Leche House in Watergate Street is probably the least altered of Chester's oldest surviving houses. It is late fifteenth century with seventeenth-century additions and its fifteenth-century hall is built over an undercroft. Its name derives from its original owner, a royal surgeon or leech, a common name for a doctor in earlier days who would use leeches as an essential part of his equipment.

Tudor House in Lower Bridge Street, carefully restored in the 1970s, was reputed to be one of the oldest houses in Chester, dating from 1503, but it is now thought that 1603 is a more likely date for its building. In Park Street the Nine Houses are in fact only six, part of what was a terrace of nine timber-framed houses, built as almshouses for the poor in 1658.

LEFT The statue of Charles I on 55 Bridge Street illustrates the king's connection with Chester during the Civil War.

BELOW Tudor House in Lower Bridge Street was thought to date from 1503, but it is now believed to have been built a century later. The gallery of a Row once went through the building, but this was altered in the eighteenth century.

ABOVE Highly decorated 55 Bridge Street, with its statue of Charles I, is a Victorian version of the timber-framed style. Steps lead up from the street to the covered walkway linking it with other shops in the Row.

BLACK-AND-WHITE BUILDINGS

A more modern interpretation of the black-and-white style is the Royal Bank of Scotland, at the corner of Frodsham Street and Foregate Street. Built in 1921, it is an extravagant version of Chester's characteristic 'magpie' buildings, with little real attempt to copy the Tudor style but achieving great splendour.

With such a fine architectural heritage, Chester has lavished a great deal of care on restoring its historic buildings. In 1981 it was the first local authority to win the European Prize for the Preservation of Historic Monuments and in 1984 and 1990 the city received the Europa Nostra medal for outstanding conservation achievements.

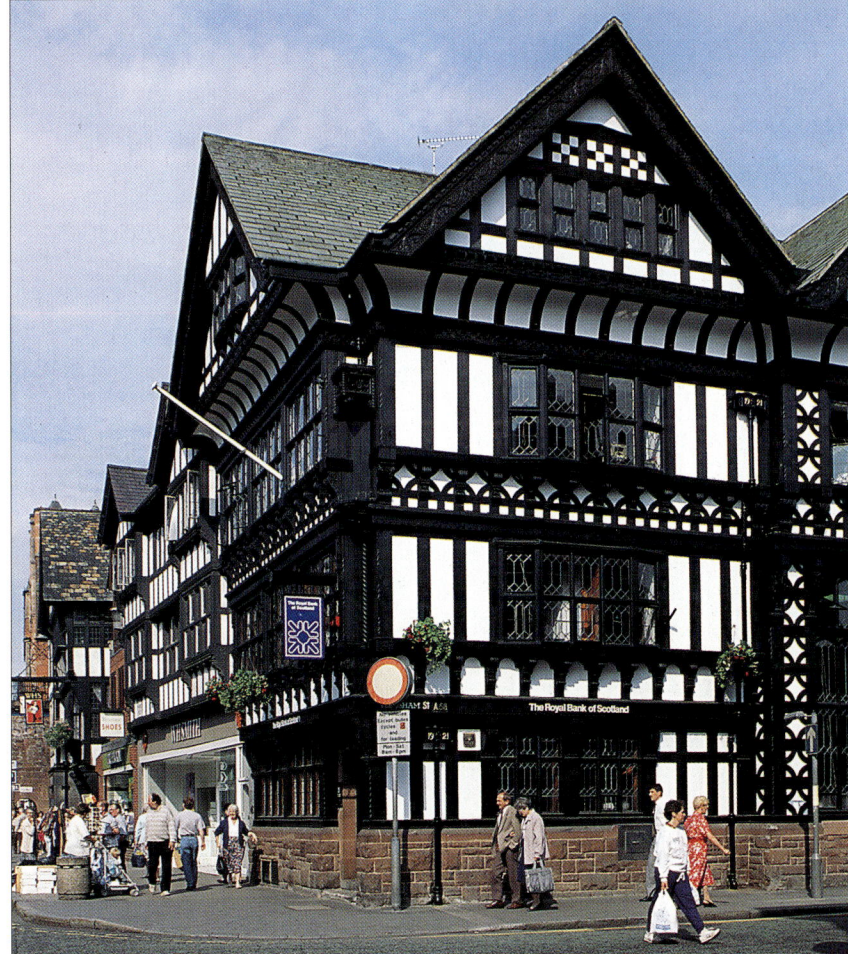

ABOVE **Only six houses are left of the original Nine Houses built as almshouses in 1658. They were restored and modernised in 1969. The timber frames rest on a sandstone base.**

LEFT **Built in 1921 and formerly the elegant District Bank, the Royal Bank of Scotland building was part of the revival of the timber-framed style which continued into the twentieth century. It was extensively restored in the 1960s. Like many of the later black-and-white buildings, it is substantially larger than the ones from the sixteenth and seventeeth centuries.**

A walk in Chester

This walk takes in part of the walls and many of Chester's most interesting features including the Rows, the Roodee, the castle, the riverside, the Roman amphitheatre, Abbey Square and the cathedral. It takes about 1½ hours but can be shortened.

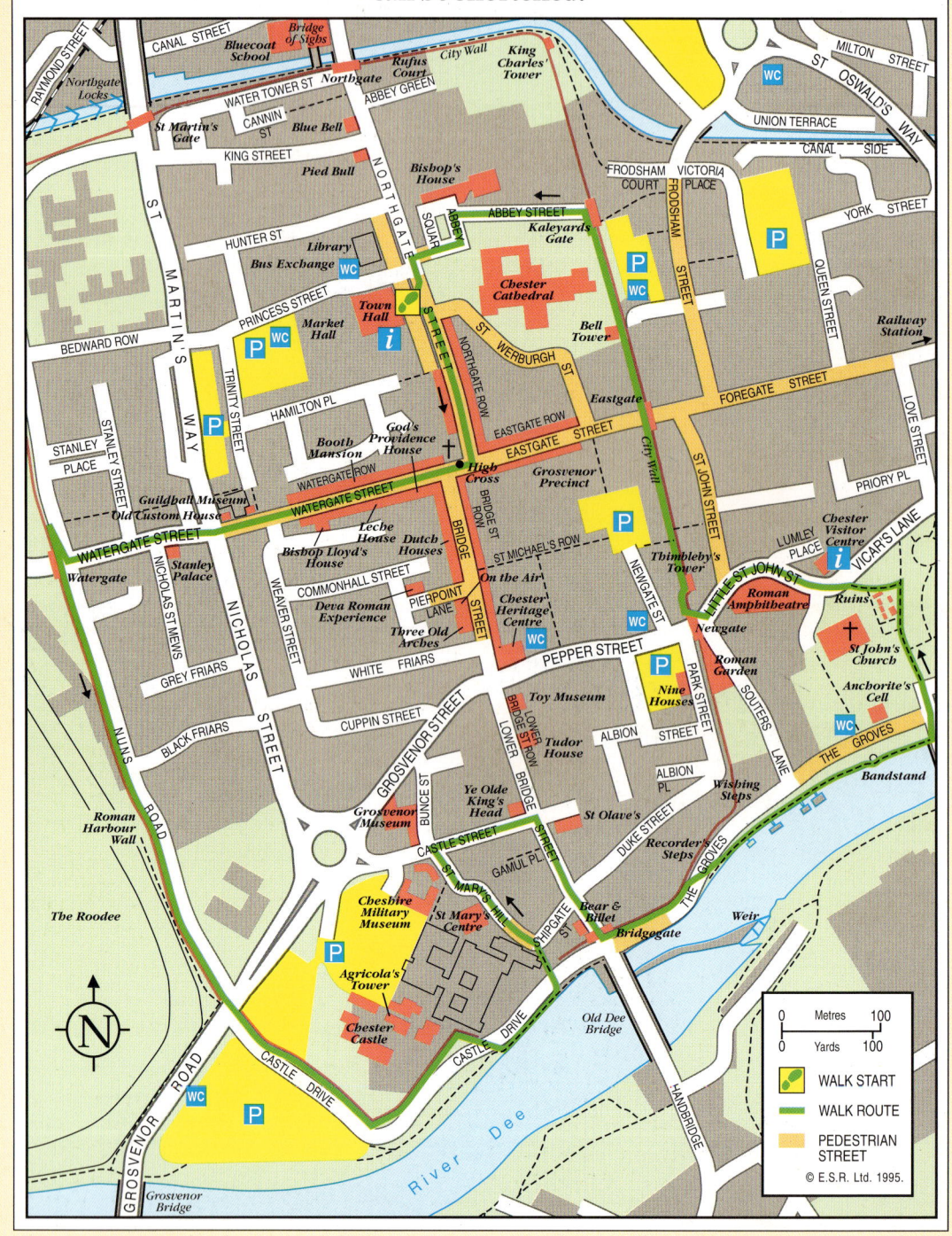

A WALK IN CHESTER

FROM the **Town Hall** (p. 21) *(right)*, facing the cathedral, turn right along Northgate Street and go past the restored Rows. Turn right into Eastgate Street (p. 16) to reach the **High Cross** (p. 16), from where black-and-white Rows radiate spectacularly in three directions.

Keep ahead along Watergate Street (pp. 16, 17), past **God's Providence House**, **Leche House** (p. 12) and then **Bishop Lloyd's House** (p. 11) with its intricate carvings. Just before the crossing, on the right, is the former custom house, part of Chester's maritime history. Cross Nicholas Street at pedestrian lights and continue ahead along Watergate Street, passing **Stanley Palace** (p. 11) *(left)*, with its interesting gables, on the left. Cross City Walls Road at more lights, turn right as far as Stanley Place, then turn left along the walls and cross over **Watergate** (p. 8). The walls overlook the unique **Roodee** (p. 27) and pass the **Roman harbour wall** and there are attractive river views.

Cross Grosvenor Road, which breaks the circuit of the city walls, by the lights, and keep ahead along the walls on the path between twin metal posts, passing stately **Chester Castle** (pp. 20, 21) on the left and with a view of **Grosvenor Bridge** *(above right)* on the right. Continue to where the path joins the road and cross to the riverside, looking across to **Old Dee Bridge** (p. 22).

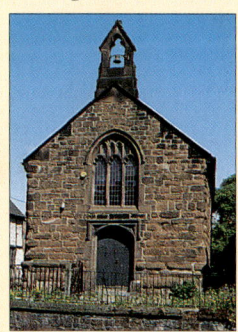

Before the bridge turn sharp left before a modern apartment block into a steep, narrow, paved and cobbled way which climbs steps alongside **St Mary's Centre**. Turn right into Castle Street past fine Georgian houses, then right into Lower Bridge Street, past the tiny former church of **St Olave's** (p. 20) *(left)*, with Gamul Place on the right. Look along cobbled Shipgate Street before reaching the **Bear and Billet** (p. 10).

Continue to **Bridgegate**, with its elegant balustrade, and climb steps on the left of the bridge up to the walls. Cross the bridge and follow the walls to the **Recorder's Steps** (p. 7) on the right. Go down them into **the Groves** (p. 22) *(right)*, and pass the bandstand and then the **Anchorite's Cell** (p. 3). Turn sharp left up steps, by the end of the suspension bridge, to **St John's Church** (p. 20) and its atmospheric ruins. Turn left past the church and continue along Little St John Street, past the **Roman amphitheatre** on the left and then the **Roman Garden** (p. 2).

At **Newgate** turn left past the bridge to climb steps onto the walls, with a good view of the **Nine Houses** (pp. 12, 13) on the left. Continue along the walls past Thimbleby's Tower and between rooftops and go up steps to the colourful **Eastgate Clock** (pp. 6, 7) *(above)*, with a superb panoramic view of the Rows. Go down steps and pass the free-standing modern bell tower and the **cathedral** (pp. 18, 19) *(right)* on the left. Then pass historic **Kaleyards Gate** (p. 8) and turn left into cobbled Georgian Abbey Street, with the cathedral on the left. In **Abbey Square** (p. 21) *(below)* there is another entrance to the cathedral, and the massive Abbey Gateway leads to Northgate Street, across which is the Town Hall.

15

STREETS AND ROWS

Streets and Rows

The central point of Chester is the High Cross, the old market cross where the lines of the Roman streets intersect. Eastgate and Watergate streets run from east to west down to the old port, following the old Via Principalis, and Northgate Street and Bridge Street run from north to south, the latter tracing the old Via Praetoria.

Chester's famous Rows, unique to the city, run along these ancient streets. They are two tiers of shops and restaurants, with galleries running above stone crypts or undercrofts. The galleries, reached by steps from the street, form an attractive shopping promenade. Originally far more extensive than they are now, there are still sections of Rows on either side of

RIGHT The High Cross, also known as St Peter's Cross and originally the site where merchants struck their bargains, is a splendid vantage point for looking at the Rows and black-and-white houses which are Chester's hallmark.

ABOVE The Rows provide an interesting form of pedestrian precinct – galleries linking properties above street level.

RIGHT Eastgate street, from Roman times a main route into the city, is now part of the pedestrianised area.

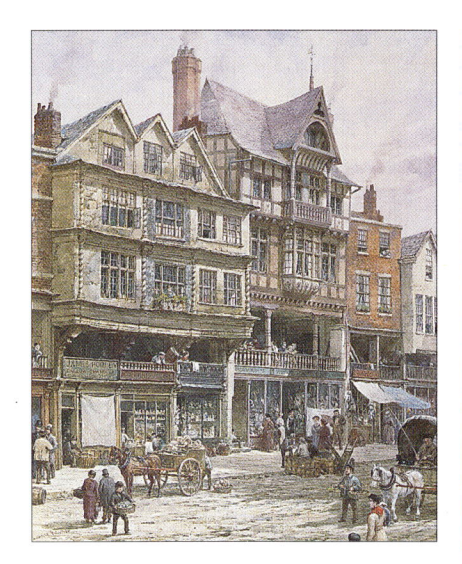

STREETS AND ROWS

ABOVE This is how the Rows looked in the nineteenth century. The painting is of a scene in Bridge Street.

Watergate, Eastgate, Northgate and Bridge streets.

Their origin is uncertain, although most authorities agree that the key period of their growth was in the thirteenth and early fourteenth centuries. The often elegantly pillared stone undercrofts were used for storage and wealthy merchants built their homes above. In some cases the upper storey became an area for smaller shops with living accomodation behind, and steps or stairs led up from the street. In time connecting galleries were built so that by the mid fourteenth century there was a continuous elevated walkway.

In later medieval times various trades moved to a particular quarter. Ironmongers Row, Cooks Row and Shoemakers Row all evolved on Northgate Street, Eastgate Street seemed to specialise in dairy products, while Fleshmongers Row was established in Watergate Street.

For a considerable period the shops on the upper level were just wooden stalls with shutters and by the eighteenth century areas around such places as 'Pepper Alley', once renowned as a 'hot spot' or trouble spot, had a dangerous reputation after dark.

Now transformed into attractive shopping arcades and walkways, the Rows are enhanced by pedestrianised streets below.

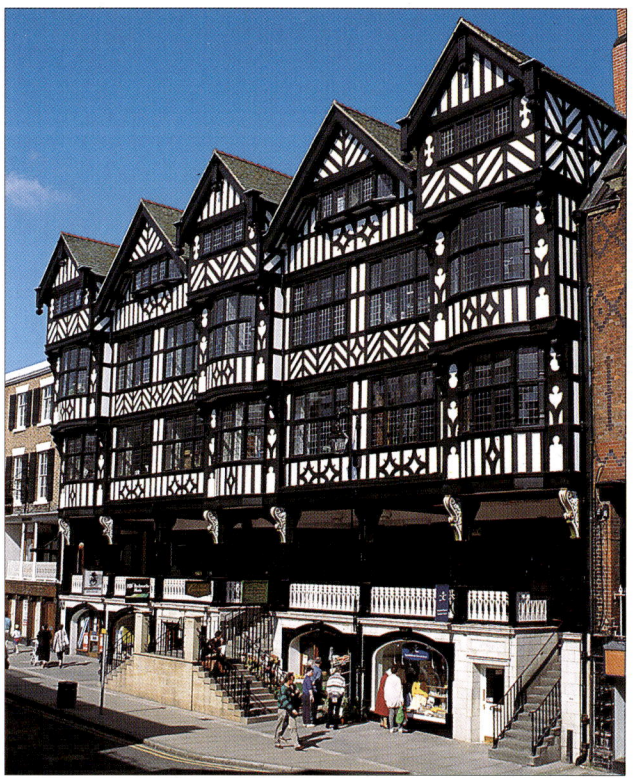

ABOVE St Michael's Buildings in Bridge Street were completed in 1910 and form an impressive entrance to the Edwardian St Michael's Row.

LEFT Elegant St Michael's Row, running at right-angles to Bridge Street and reached by steps from it, was built in 1910 as a covered shopping street at an upper level. It leads to the Grosvenor shopping precinct.

Chester Cathedral

In the heart of Chester lies its great red sandstone cathedral with its towering nave, Norman arch in the north transept and exquisite wood carving in the choir. The beautiful cloisters recall its monastic past.

A church was established on the site soon after AD 907. Dedicated to St Werburgh, the Anglo-Saxon princess and abbess, it contained her relics and soon became a focal point for medieval pilgrimage.

In 1092 a Benedictine abbey was founded there and the monastery remained for nearly 500 years, growing in power and prosperity. At the dissolution of the monasteries in 1540 the abbey church became Chester's cathedral.

The lady chapel dates from the thirteenth century and the immense south transept from the fourteenth. The cathedral's last great building period starting in medieval times was from 1484 to 1537 when parts of the nave, the south-west porch, the west front and the top storey of the central tower were constructed. Its many remarkable features include the superb choir stalls dating from 1390 which reveal masterly carving and inventiveness.

In many parts of the cathedral seventeenth-, eighteenth- and early-nineteenth-century restorations have been overlaid by Victorian craftmanship, an essential preservation measure since so much

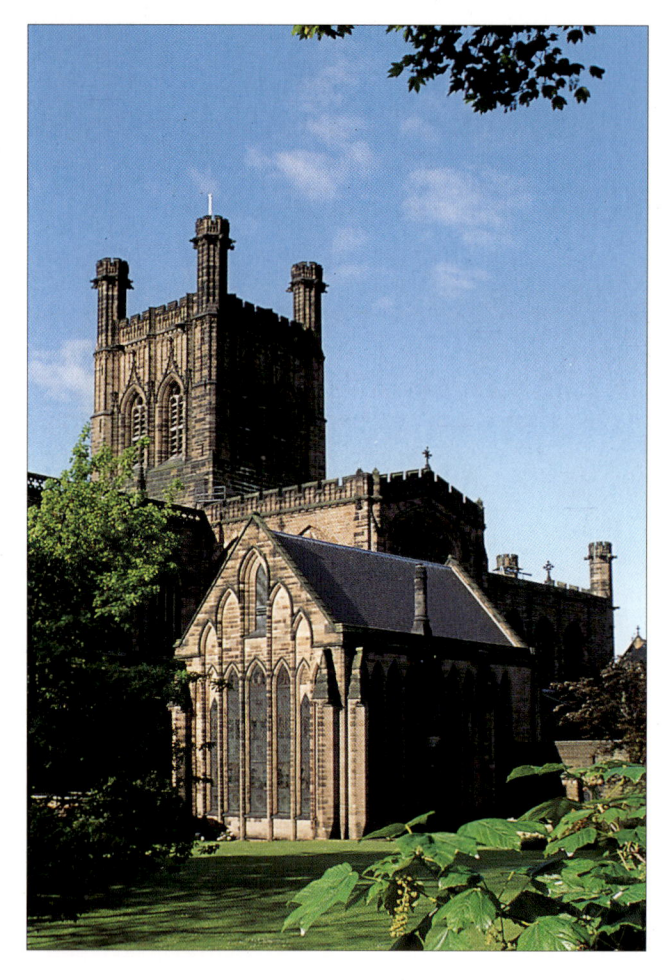

BELOW The red sandstone Chester Cathedral is a dramatic sight, seen here from the city walls, with the chapter house in the foreground. This northern side of the cathedral has the well-preserved monastic buildings which give an idea of how the medieval abbey would have appeared.

ABOVE St Werburgh's shrine, which dates from about 1320, once housed the saint's bones but these were removed to safety by the monks in 1540. Pilgrims used to kneel at the shrine to be close to the relics.

CHESTER CATHEDRAL

RIGHT **The fourteenth-century choir stalls have some of the finest of misericords. This one illustrates a legend about St Werburgh restoring to life one of her geese eaten by a servant. It shows the bones on a plate, the bird flying away and the servant confessing.**

BELOW **A rich symphony of intricate carving, dazzling in its virtuosity, is formed by the canopies in the choir. This 'lacework' complements the charm and wit of the choir stalls below.**

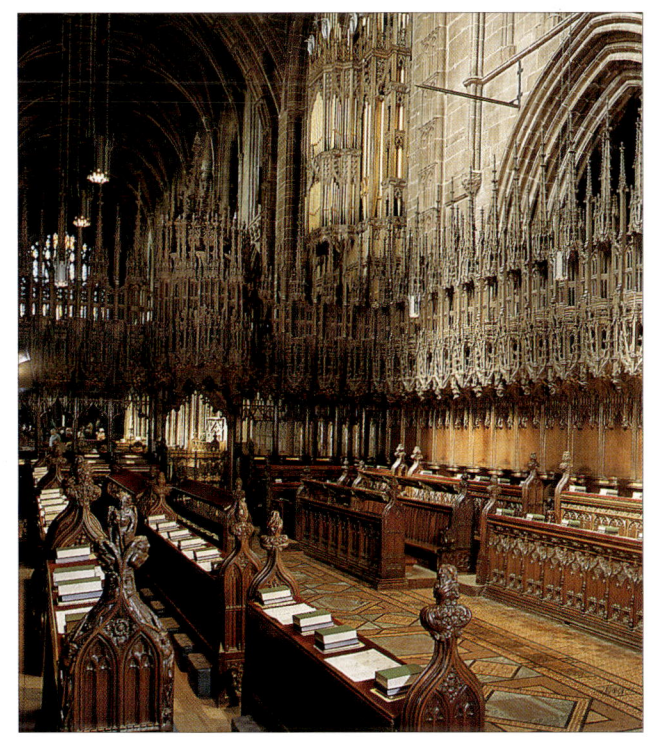

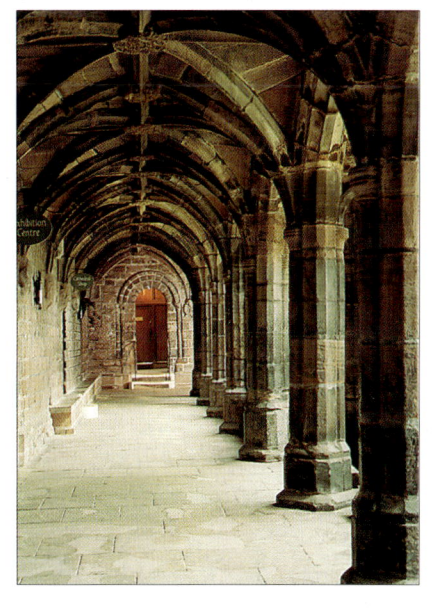

ABOVE **The twelfth-century cloisters were largely rebuilt in the sixteenth century.**

BELOW **Some fine stained glass is contained in the elegant chapter house.**

of the soft red sandstone had become badly eroded. The organ loft, choir screen and many of the stained-glass windows belong to this later period.

The monastic buildings on the north side of the cathedral, built round the cloisters mainly in the twelfth and thirteenth centuries, are among the best preserved in the country. The monks' refectory has a complete stone wall pulpit, approached by an arcaded flight of steps.

In 1974 the Addleshaw Tower was completed as the first detached bell-tower built for an English cathedral since the fifteenth century.

HISTORIC BUILDINGS

Historic buildings

The great charm of Chester's historic buildings lies in their tremendous variety, with buildings from all centuries adding to or complementing the architecture of preceding periods.

St John's Church was for a time Chester's first cathedral. Built on the site of a seventh-century Anglo-Saxon church, it was a cathedral in the eleventh century, became a parish church after the dissolution of the monasteries in 1540, and later part of the building was allowed to fall into decay and now survives only as ruins.

The church has a massive, largely Norman nave and its special features include a fine medieval wall painting of St John the Baptist.

Tiny St Olave's in Lower Bridge Street is dedicated to St Olave, a Norwegian king who was killed in 1030 after fighting for the English. Built in the twelfth century, it was restored as a school in 1860. An extremely rare survival of a stone front of a medieval house is the Three Old Arches in Bridge Street which has been dated as early 1274.

BELOW Chester Castle was radically rebuilt by Thomas Harrison, who won a competition in 1785 to provide new county buildings on the site. The shirehall, barracks and armoury were all built in neo-classical style. This is the entrance to what is now the Law Courts and County Hall.

BELOW St John's Church, once Chester's cathedral, dates from Norman times and its magnificent Norman arches indicate the ambitious scale of the project. Part of it later fell into decay and among the ruins are some Saxon crosses from the previous church on the site.

HISTORIC BUILDINGS

The original Chester Castle was Norman, and it was rebuilt and modified in the thirteenth and fourteenth centuries, but the only remains are Agricola's Tower, the stone ramparts and a twelfth-century chapel. Its rebuilding in the eighteenth century was in elegant Greek Revival style by Thomas Harrison. The buildings now house courts, council offices and a museum.

Typical of Georgian Chester is Abbey Square, laid out in the mid 1750s on the site of the abbey's medieval bakehouse and brewery. Two terraces of elegant houses are built around the green and a cobbled court.

The high-Victorian Town Hall of 1869 which dominates the square it overlooks has a tower 160 feet (48 m) high and ornate decoration both inside and out.

ABOVE **Abbey Square**, with its Georgian brick terraces, can be reached through the splendid Abbey Gateway on Northgate Street. Its cobbled streets with inlaid 'wheelers', or flat stones, helped to make carriage journeys more comfortable.

Thomas Hughes (1822–96), writer, philanthropist and author of the classic account of public-school life *Tom Brown's Schooldays*, made his home in Chester when he was appointed as county court judge in 1882. After three years in rented houses – at first at elegant Georgian Stanley Place and then at Sandowne Terrace – he had Uffington House built and lived there until he died eleven years later. It is now 20 Dee Hills Park.

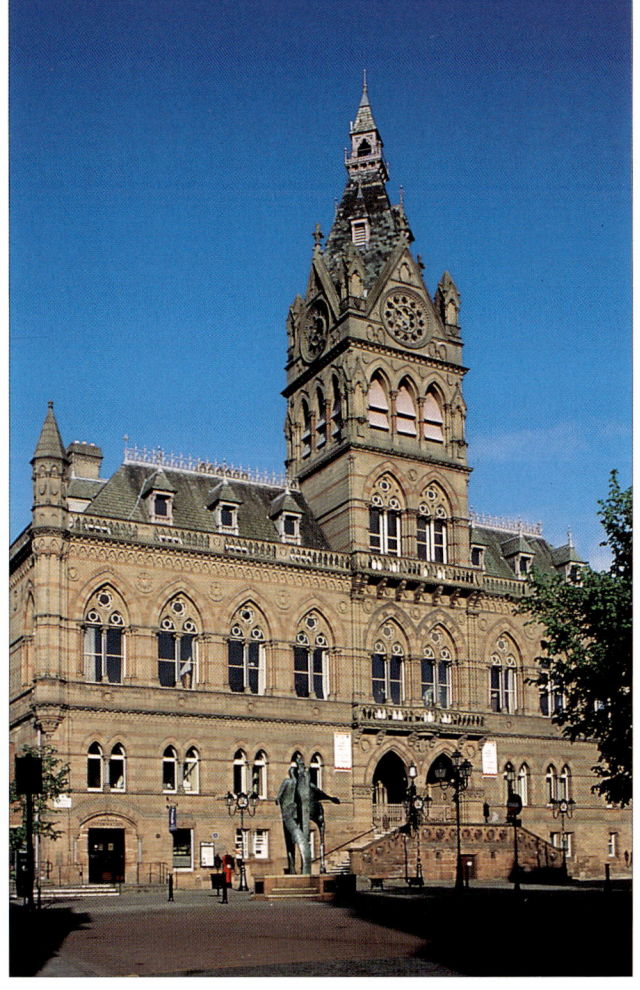

LEFT **Chester's Town Hall**, built of grey sandstone by William H. Lynn in 1869 at the then enormous cost of £40,000, was officially opened by the future Edward VII, the then Prince of Wales and Earl of Chester.

RIVER AND CANAL

River and canal

BELOW **The Groves riverside promenade is named after the groups of trees which shade it. It is a pleasant place to stroll, watch the numerous boats on the river and listen to a band in the bandstand.**

Nowadays the River Dee at Chester is thronged with colourful pleasure boats, with the delicate outline of the suspension bridge framing the scene.

But for centuries Chester was the principal port of north-west England, with strong trading links with Ireland. By the fourteenth century goods traded through the port included iron, tar, oil, wax, sugar, cloth and hides for tanning, and a wine trade was established with France and Spain. The harbour had its own court, the Portmoot, to regulate maritime business, and there were even cheese wharfs for the famous Cheshire cheeses. Watergate Street, lined with warehouses, led through

BELOW **Seven-arched Old Dee Bridge was until the nineteenth century the only bridge over the Dee at Chester. It dates from 1387 and replaced earlier wooden bridges. One is mentioned in Domesday Book and records indicate that in the thirteenth and fourteenth centuries bridges were destroyed by floods.**

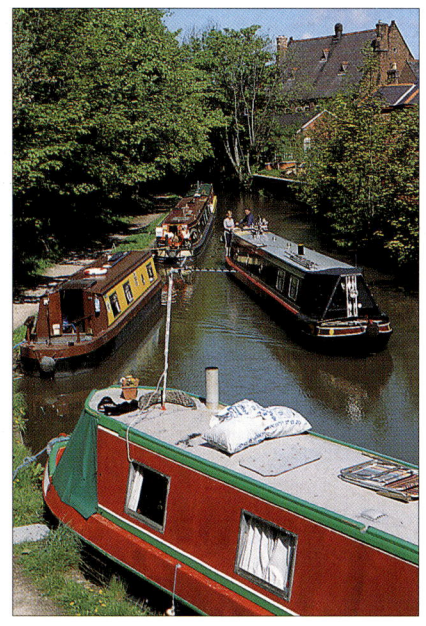

RIVER AND CANAL

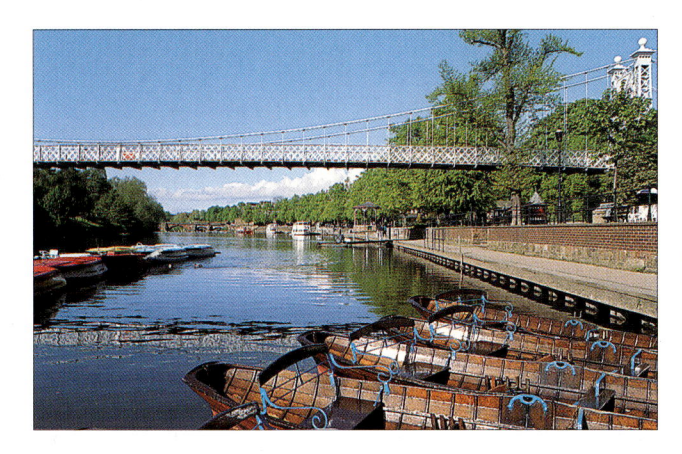

ABOVE **The elegant iron suspension bridge spanning the River Dee is a footbridge rebuilt in 1923 in a similar style to the original bridge of 1852.**

BELOW **A trip in a brightly painted traditional narrow-boat is a relaxing way to enjoy such sights as the city walls, the dramatic gorge by the Bridge of Sighs and some of Chester's industrial past.**

George Frederick Handel (1685–1759), composer of the celebrated oratorio *Messiah*, in 1742 waited in Blossom's Hotel in St John Street for some time for favourable winds for his crossing to Dublin for the première of this great work. He whiled away the time by rehearsing choruses from the work with local citizens in Chester Cathedral, who must have enormously relished this unexpected chance to participate in such a vivid dramatic work.

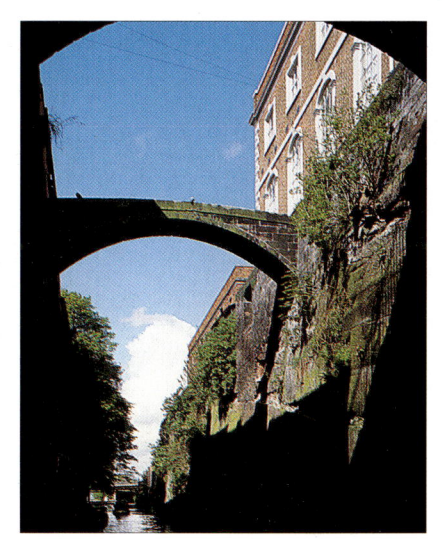

LEFT **The Bridge of Sighs over the deep canal cutting was built for prisoners from the gaol in the Northgate to attend the chapel at the Bluecoat School. Condemned men were also led across for last rites in the chapel.**

the Watergate down to the old harbour area. But as early as the fifteenth century Chester's trade was threatened by the gradual silting up of the River Dee, although the city's ship-building industry, prominent from medieval times, was still more important than Liverpool's as late as 1810.

A weir was built on the river in Norman times, and in the sixteenth century its waters powered up to eleven mills: six for grinding, two to lift water to the city and three for fulling cloth. In the early twentieth century its waters were used to provide hydro-electricity. The Dee has been famous since Saxon times for its salmon fishing, which is still a popular activity.

Chester's canal was opened in 1775, soon linking Chester with the Cheshire salt mines and the Midland canal network, and by 1797 there was another link from Chester via the Ellesmere Canal to Ellesmere Port on the Mersey.

The canal area has now been restored with warehouses and mills converted to pubs and restaurants, and there is a pleasant walk along the towpath into the heart of the city.

MUSEUMS

Museums

Visitors to Chester can stroll along a reconstructed Victorian street – complete with sounds and smells of the period – peer into various archaeological layers, tune in to Churchill's wartime broadcasts and view the largest collection of 'Matchbox' toys in the world. For the range of interest provided by the city's museums is wide.

The Grosvenor Museum has a remarkable collection of stone altars and memorial tablets which has won an award for its stylish layout. Roman objects, natural and local history displays, paintings and drawings of the city and a collection of Chester silverware can all be seen there. At the Castle Street Period House a series of furnished period rooms give insight into life in the city in Georgian and Victorian times.

The Rows in Victorian times can be experienced in an atmospheric reconstruction – complete with cobbled street, sounds and smells – at the Chester Visitor Centre.

There are reconstructions of Roman streets and a simulated trip on a galley at the Dewa Roman Experience, a small museum based on a major archaeological dig into the foundations of what may have been a Roman tribune's house in Chester. Visitors have an opportunity to handle archaeological discoveries.

The siege of Chester during the Civil War is described in a small exhibition at King Charles' Tower, and the Cheshire Military Museum has a collection of regimental

ABOVE **Chester is known for its silver, of which there is a fine collection in the Grosvenor Museum. These two large silver gilt cups were presented for Chester Races in 1814 and 1815, and the gold tumbler in 1776. The city still has working silversmiths and it had an assay office until 1962.**

RIGHT **The Georgian room is one of a series of furnished rooms in the Castle Street Period House. The rooms show furnishings and costumes from 1680 to 1920. This scene from the year 1780 is complete with a period Worcester tea service.**

MUSEUMS

LEFT Soak up the atmosphere in this convincing life-size recreation of a Victorian street, complete with sounds and smells, at the Chester Visitor Centre. The centre is housed in a former school built in Victorian times.

BELOW The On the Air museum tells the story of broadcasting from its early days, and has vintage wireless and television sets, a mock television studio and 'hands on' exhibits.

RIGHT This Chad Valley tin-plate van from the Toy Museum is regarded as a classic example of English toymaking in the 1950s.

memorabilia, uniforms and weaponry from the eighteenth century to the present day.

Chester Heritage Centre, housed in St Michael's Church, was Britain's first architectural heritage centre. It has a video presentation of Chester's history with exhibitions describing the city's conservation programme.

Of more general interest is the Toy Museum which houses the largest collection of 'Matchbox' vehicles in the world as well as many other delightful period toys and games. And the On the Air museum tells the story of broadcasting from the golden age of wireless to today's satellite TV.

25

FESTIVALS

Festivals

Chester's river is such an important part of its history that it is hardly surprising that water festivals feature in the city's annual events. The city also has a two-week music festival and every five years mystery plays, powerful renderings of biblical stories, are performed there. All events are announced at the High Cross as they have been for centuries by the strikingly costumed Town Crier, who reads proclamations from April to September – but no longer promotes such events as bear baiting and cock fighting!

An exciting and moving spectacle, the Chester mystery plays were performed by medieval craft guilds in the streets, originally on carts, each guild producing the biblical story which seemed most appropriate to its trade. Now they are performed every five years in the cathedral grounds.

Chester races have a superb and unusual setting on the 'soup plate' on the Roodee, the site of the ancient Roman harbour. It is a traditional and colourful occasion, with the season starting in early May and finishing in late September.

Chester Regatta has a 260-year-old tradition as an annual rowing competition in early June. The course follows the Dee from the Red House to the Canoe Club, with rowing events on the Saturday and canoeing

LEFT In the summer at 12 noon and again at 2 pm every day except Sundays and Mondays proclamations are read at the High Cross where the four main streets converge.

RIGHT Every five years over a three-week period Chester's mystery plays take place, complete with processions beforehand.

FESTIVALS

LEFT Chester's racecourse on the Roodee is one of the oldest in the country. Its principal meeting is held in May and the Chester Cup is the main prize.

BELOW Featuring a procession through the city centre, the annual Lord Mayor's Show provides participants and onlookers with a feast of fun and entertainment.

on the Sunday. For those who take their water sports less seriously, there is plenty of fun and high spirits in the River Carnival and Raft Race in early July, with a flotilla of themed rafts, bands and sideshows.

Regimental parades and massed bands provide colour and ceremony on a summer evening at Chester Castle for Beating the Retreat. In late July Chester Summer Music Festival caters for musical tastes from classical recitals to jazz and sophisticated late-night cabaret.

LEFT Chester Summer Music Festival has some outstanding concerts. Here Mark Jordan, playing the Northumbrian pipes, is seen with the composer and conductor Sir Peter Maxwell Davies and the BBC Philharmonic Orchestra at the première of Cross Lane Fair, a piece specially composed for the soloist.

FURTHER INFORMATION

Further information

Details are correct at the time of writing but may be changed.

Band concerts
The Bandstand, The Groves.
May–Sep Sun usually 3 and 6.30.

Boat trips
River boats from The Groves.
Canal boats from the Mill Hotel, Milton Street.

Castle Street Period House
Attractive period furnishings.
See Grosvenor Museum.

Cheshire Military Museum
Display of weapons and uniforms.
Chester Castle, off Grosvenor Road (Tel: 01244 327617).
Open daily 9–5, Admission charge.

Chester Cathedral
Very fine carvings in choir and well-preserved monastic cloisters.
Abbey Street (Tel: 01244 324756).
Open daily 7–6.30. Admission free.

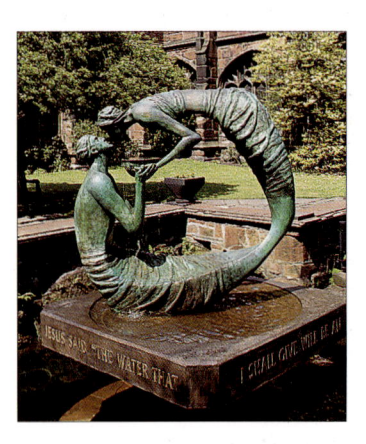

ABOVE **This striking modern sculpture by Stephen Broadbent, in the cloister garden of Chester Cathedral, is entitled *The Water of Life*. It was installed in 1994.**

ABOVE **Mother and daughter are delightful evidence of Chester Zoo's success in breeding orang-utans. The zoo is proud of its conservation programme.**

Chester Heritage Centre
Good insights into conservation programme.
St Michael's Church, Bridge Street Row (Tel: 01244 317948).
Open Mon–Sat 11–5, Sun 12–5. Admission charge.

Chester Visitor Centre
Reconstruction of Chester's Victorian Rows.
Vicar's Lane (Tel: 01244 318916).
Open Apr–Oct daily 9–6. Nov–Mar daily 9–5. Admission free.

Chester Zoo
Set in 110 acres of splendid gardens.
Upton-by-Chester, 2 miles (3 km) north of city off A41 (Tel: 01244 380280). Open daily 10–6/6.30/7 (last entry 4.30/5/5.30) summer, 10–4.30/5/5.30 (last entry 3.30/4) winter. Closed Christmas Day. Admission charge.

Dewa Roman Experience
Interesting archaeological dig on view.
Pierpoint Lane, off Bridge Street (Tel: 01244 343407). Open daily 9–6.

ABOVE **At the Dewa Roman Experience this cart in front of a mural of a Roman street scene helps to recreate the atmosphere of Roman times.**